Why Your Website Doesn't Make Money

& how it can...

By Paul Mannet

siterelauncher.com

ISBN 10: 1490595406
Copyright © 2013 Rum Point Digital, Inc.
Port Washington, NY 11050

Contents

Preface: Purpose Of This Book

This book is designed to help you deal with the toughest obstacle that business owners, bloggers and entrepreneurs run into when they're trying to succeed in the digital world. It's the nagging problem of having a website that's one to three years old, and just does not seem to be making any money for you, either directly or indirectly.

I've been an editor, salesperson and publisher at various points in my career. But for the past 15 years, I've worked as a digital project manager and business analyst, advising everyone from companies with 100 websites to individuals trying to create a first blog. It's been an alternately fascinating and horrifying experience – horrifying because I've watched so many site owners make a few basic mistakes over and over again, derailing their chances of online success.

Not everyone starts a blog or website to earn a profit. But before too long, everyone comes to the same realization: it's too much effort to keep a website going if it's not going to make any real money.

I actually think this problem has grown worse because it's now so cheap and easy to launch a site. Low cost "build a site" packages offered by hosting companies, dirt cheap domain names and free CMS options like Wordpress have all made it possible to press a few buttons and see your new site live on the web in the time it takes to make a cup of coffee. You hardly have to think about it.

As a result, people have a real tendency to "shoot now and aim later" on website launches. And while I know from experience that you don't need to be a business genius to have a website that earns revenue, you do need to have clear picture in your mind of how and why a person visiting your site will result in a payment to you. If you're hazy on that, success will be a real long shot.

One rock solid truth holds true for Google AdSense, affiliate marketing, ecommerce and all the other approaches you'll find covered here: they can either be great money makers or total losers – depending on whether or not you know how to use them correctly. If I steer you away from jumping into any of these approaches without stopping to think them through, I believe I will save you a great deal of aggravation and wasted time.

I've made a particular effort to talk about best website approaches for small businesses and for professional offices that don't actually sell anything online. The Internet poses particular challenges if you're one of these, but it can also hold more opportunity than you realize.

This book won't turn you into a professional web developer. But it will equip you to ask smarter questions, to better understand why some people out there are making money online and prevent you from sounding "out of it" about digital. That last one is particularly important if you're hiring a designer or other expert to work on your site.

Whether you hope to build a full scale business or simply make some extra money on the side, I hope you'll use this book as a tool to create smarter sites, email newsletters, mobile applications and online marketing plans in the shortest time possible, so you can prosper in the digital world.

- *Paul Mannet*

Disclaimer

Throughout this book I've recommended a few applications and courses you can download free or purchase. These recommendations are based purely on my belief in their quality. I do not have any business relationship with the companies that produce them, and I won't benefit in any way if you follow through and purchase any of them. I've mentioned relatively few, because I don't want to endorse anything that I haven't actually used myself.

1 "One Year Burnout Sites"

"The real problem is not whether machines think but whether men do." – B.F. Skinner

You sit staring at your traffic report, trying to figure out what the problem is. Your site looks good and you're getting more visitors all the time, but your revenue is almost nothing. Google ads pay you less than $100. a month and your affiliate commissions are barely enough to pay for a nice dinner now and then. You're starting to give in to the fact that your website is not on a path to success, unless something changes.

You're in good company. I can report to you that large businesses, startups backed by venture capitalists, young and old entrepreneurs and business owners on Main

Street across the country have all worked themselves into the same position. In most cases, they've wasted time and money, and potentially doomed themselves to failure by not learning some basic concepts involved in executing a site.

The most dramatic example I've seen in big-company environments is the "one year burnout site." That's the process of spending a hair-raising amount of money and effort to create a site, only to decide one year later that it's a disaster that already needs to be rebuilt. I can tell you, in fact, that I've seen companies spend six figures on developing a site and decide it's a disaster *even before it's launched.*

The best way to avoid your own online disaster is to make a point of learning some basics about the technology of the web and about the design approaches that actually drive results. As you do that, you'll start to find it easier to put aside the things that don't matter and focus on what can really work for your online business.

Easy Mark

It's particularly important to educate yourself about the web if you're going to hire anyone to do design work or help you out with the tech setup of your site.

There tend to be two kinds of people out there who will do website work for the blogger or small business owner: the ones who know exactly what they're doing, and the ones who have no idea what they're doing. Both of them pose real risks to you.

If you're talking with a very knowledgeable developer, you don't want to come off sounding like a digital nincompoop. Particularly in the small business sector, the internet remains a bit of a wild west where you'll encounter very sharp people who would love to charge you an outrageous price. Mangling digital terminology, not knowing how your current site works or not having a clear goal will all telegraph to them that you're an easy mark.

The other type, which you'll encounter more often, is the web designer who has only a limited knowledge of one aspect of web development, but would like you to hire them to re-do your site completely. Graphic designers who can make your site look pretty but will make a disaster out of its mechanics are particularly plentiful. If you don't know the right questions to ask to eliminate this type of person, you'll find yourself three months down the road with a half-built site, and a need to hire someone else to fix the mess that's been created – a very, very common situation.

To make yourself a smarter site owner, start by taking a deep breath and learning some concepts I believe most "non-techies" can grasp that dictate whether or not you'll get a real benefit from your site.

2 Talking The Talk – Digital Terms You Don't Want To Mangle

"The Internet is a great way to get on the net."
– Senator Bob Dole

You'll have a better chance of translating your needs into an actual website design if you learn some simple terminology. Here are some key terms and acronyms you should understand whether you're going it alone or hiring someone to do your site for you.

"Hits" Are A Sure Miss

If you want people to think your web knowledge is 10 years out of date, a great way to do so is to talk about getting "hits" on your website.

When someone opens a page on your site, it generates a pageview, not a hit. A hit is different. Every web page you see has a header, a footer and other layout elements. And every one of those elements will register a hit to your server each time a single pageview is generated. So you can have dozens of hits on one pageview.

Hits are not in any way a measurement of how much traffic you have or how many individuals are visiting your site. If you're talking about site traffic, talk in terms of pageviews. Confusing pageviews with hits conveys that you're not familiar with basic web measurement tools like Google Analytics, Statcounter or Omniture (which we'll cover later).

Users Should Be Unique

Most site owners want a basic measurement of how big their population of users or readers is. Traditional publishers are used to having a circulation list, and they look for a similar online metric.

"Users" or "visitors" are the terms that cover

this, depending on what program you use to measure web traffic. But you should be aware that the most widely accepted measurement of how many human beings visit your site is not simply users, because web analytics tools can report one person again and again if the measurement is done over a too long a time.

It's easier to "unduplicate" the visits of a single user if you measure one month at a time. Don't worry about why – it has to do with how web analytics software works. Just remember that the accepted term is "monthly unique users" or just "monthly uniques" (unless you're using the "visitors" terminology). It's the term that best gauges the size of your site's user base.

"Visits," by the way, is the term that measures the number of times someone comes to your website. So one user or visitor can generate an unlimited number of visits.

Social Media Speak
Lots of nouns have become verbs on the web,

particularly in the area of social media:

Blogomania
DO say: "I blogged about the event" or "I wrote a post about it."
DON'T say: "I wrote a blog about the event." That would infer that you created an entire blog or website about the event.

Facebook
DO say: "I'm on Facebook" or "I use Facebook."
DON'T say: "I've got a Facebook." There's only one Facebook, and it's a massive network. You can use it or be on it, but you can't have it.
Additionally, it's fine to say "I'll friend you" or "he friended me."

Twitter
DO say: "I tweeted that" or "I tweeted about that."
DON'T say: "I twittered that."

Googling

DO say "I Googled you." It's simply become the fast form way of saying "I looked up information about you on Google."

SEO Terms Of Confusion

Search engine optimization, called "SEO" by just about every web professional, basically means organizing the information on your site pages to maximize their attractiveness to search engines. Above all else, be aware that getting good rankings in Google is an unpredictable process where Google can – and frequently does – change the rules in a heartbeat. Anybody who tells you that you'll always be on the first page of Google results if you do exactly what they say – and there are tons of these people out there – should be looked on very warily. SEO is an area where you need to use common sense and avoid sneaky "black hat" tricks that can get your site banned by the search engines.

That said, you'll want to know these terms as you discuss your site's SEO plan:

Keywords

Google is primarily a machine, not a person, and it needs markers to help people who are searching find what they're looking for. The most basic of these are keywords or keyword phrases. If you're a content producer, which could include anyone from a news writer to a professional office, the right keywords will tend to occur naturally in the articles or pages you create. If you are a retailer or affiliate, you will need to be more strategic about integrating specific keyword phrases into your shopping and promotional pages to draw people to your site.

If you sell printers, for example, it will be OK for you to have the keyword "printer" in your content and meta tags (meta terms explained below), but you'll probably want to focus on more specific terms like "Epson printers" or "Epson Artisan 130 printer" (assuming you sell those products) to win in the search results and bring actual shoppers to your site. This actually incorporates two concepts, "long tail" and "terms of purchase intent."

Long Tail

An approach of using many very specific keyword phrases. You can, potentially, score higher in search results for terms like "two sided color invitations" than you can for just "custom printing" because so many more sites will be competing for the latter phrase. It's a widely accepted strategy to compete for lots of "long tail" phrases instead of just a few major ones that are tough to win for. If you have a law office, you're more likely to score highly in Google for a long tail term like "Town of North Hempstead property closings" than a broad term like "real estate lawyer."

Terms of Purchase Intent

A fairly basic idea, familiar to most online direct marketers. It simply means that a term like "best replacement tires for 2009 Ford pickup" is more likely to bring you real shoppers than a broader term like "trucking," which may only bring you lots of Grateful Dead fans. If you think about it, it's usually not hard to figure who which kinds of terms signal that people are in the actual process of shopping. Most site owners will want to win for those terms more than any others.

SERP

Acronym for "search engine results pages." Web people will often talk about how you're "scoring in the SERPs," which means whether you're coming in #1 or #50 in Google for specific keyword terms.

Meta Tags or Meta Information

Keywords, mentioned above, actually appear in two places: in the body of your page copy and in the "meta tags." Within the code of any good web page is a meta information section that includes a page title, keywords and a description. On Wordpress and just about all other CMS's, you're prompted to fill these in before you publish a post or article.

Because so many people have tried to play games with meta keywords, Google doesn't look at them anymore. But the page title – not the headline but the one in the meta information – and the description are both critical because they help Google find you and get people to click to you.

When your pages come up in search results, the page title and description are what people are almost always going to see. A title and description work as your advertisement in the search results. The better they are, the greater the chance that someone will click through your site from the SERPS. (If you want to see how competitors are handling these, right click on any web page, then scroll and click "view page source." Near the top of the window that pops up, you will see their title, keywords and description.)

SEO, by the way, is another of those terms that's become both noun and verb. Accepted usages include:
"We have to SEO these pages."
"She's an SEO" (meaning she's a search engine optimization professional).
"We need to teach the editors SEO."

Behind The Curtain: What's Running Your Site

The Content Management System or "CMS"

Back in the dark ages of the 1990's, many of us made websites by creating a bunch of pages in an HTML editor like Dreamweaver, and then just downloading them to wherever our website was hosted.

But today, virtually all blogs and websites are run by a content management system, referred to as "the CMS." To understand the idea of a CMS, you need to know that the pages on your website don't actually exist anywhere as complete things. They live in pieces – images, words and layout elements – that are only organized into a page at the instant a user clicks to one of your urls. What puts them all together is the CMS, with the help of a guide called a stylesheet.

Some of the most popular CMS systems are Wordpress, Drupal, Joomla and DotNetNuke. Companies that have an in-house development staff will often take the code from a large "open source" (free) one like Drupal and use it as a foundation to build out their own unique CMS. But Drupal is a brutally difficult thing to learn. Most smaller publishers use Wordpress, which is also free, but a good deal easier to use than Drupal.

How good your CMS is will determine whether your site is a dream to work with or a constant pain in the neck. If you're working with a developer, make sure he or she takes you through the process of putting up a page on your site, so you can see if it's a smooth process or not.

It's in your interest to design a layout that will serve all the different sections you envision for your site. That's because, once your stylesheet and your CMS are up and running, it's hard to change any one part of the site to look different from the other pages. A CMS gives you lots of advantages, but it also creates a certain inflexibility.

*Tip for small publishers: I advise against

using Blogger from Google or wordpress.com, which are both free, to start a site. If you become successful, you run into a problem of not really owning your site or your url. Better to try one of the "easy website" packages available on most hosting services, download Wordpress to your hosting account from wordpress.org, or try a CMS like sitesell.com, which also includes email newsletter functions and lots of other goodies (it costs about $300. per year).

Hosting

All those words and pictures that make up your website have to be stored somewhere – on a machine called a server. Your hosting service runs those servers, and can provide lots of other extras for your site.

If you're in a big company, you probably won't get involved in discussing hosting because your tech department will already have a contract with a hosting provider. If you're an individual publisher, choosing a hosting service is a bigger issue. There actually isn't a great deal of difference between what hosting companies provide or what they charge nowadays, but there's a huge difference in how much customer service they give when something goes wrong, and something always goes wrong. Two hosting companies I've been happy with are 1and1 and Bluehost. I would not recommend Dotster.

RSS
Nobody is completely sure what this stands for, but most seem to accept that it's an abbreviation for "really simple syndication." You definitely want to make sure your site has an RSS feed, because it sends out a very stripped-down version of your site pages with no graphic design elements wrapped around them. That's important to readers who want to see your site on smartphones and other mobile devices (you can see what the RSS for most sites look like by just typing in "/rss" or "/feed" at the end of their urls). If you read the apps from New York Times, Wall Street Journal or just about any other news source,

the information is being pulled into your app and updated constantly through RSS feeds. An RSS feed from your site can also help you disseminate your content to anyone who wants to follow what you're writing about (lots of journalists use RSS readers to stay up to date with lots of news sources), which can help bring you lots of valuable links. RSS feeds are part of most basic site packages today. If your site doesn't have a feed, you can create one for free at feedburner.google.com/.

HTML

It may seem a bit unnecessary to mention HTML, because the rise of rich text editors in most online publishing systems has made it less necessary to know about. But HTML is a basic building block of every website, and there continue to be reasons why it's good to have at least a minimal skill level with it.

HTML stands for "hypertext markup language." What does that mean? Well, if you're terribly old like me, you remember computers that showed nothing but ugly green screens with letters on them. The reason you don't see that any more is HTML. It's a coding language that "marks up" the data coming into your computer so that it will look pretty in Explorer, Chrome, Firefox, Safari or any other browser you're using to view the web. If you right click in most browsers and hit "view source" you'll see that, behind the scenes in any page you view, there's a mass of HTML code.

In HTML, a "tag" like <b> makes your browser show a word in **bold**. Another tag calls up a photo and shows it to you in a particular location on a page. Other tags dictate the column structure of a page while still others determine the background colors of a site.

As I've said, you can get away without writing much HTML nowadays. But there are two reasons why it's good to cultivate at least a basic knowledge of it anyway:

1) You'll often need it to fix problems on your site, move things around a little

bit, or put in things that don't come with your original theme or design.

2) Knowing it can allow you to quickly see lots of information about your competitors. Viewing the HTML source code of someone else's site, which you can easily do online, can quickly tell you what ad serving system they're using, what analytics program they run, and, potentially, many other things like who their designer was and where they got certain widgets and other cool things.

3 Ten Key Website Mistakes You Want To Avoid

"Design is not just what it looks like and feels like. Design is how it works." — Steve Jobs

We all tend to get fascinated by technology. But in truth, tech is only a part of the website design process. The other part, which is usually tougher, is the job of fully thinking through how a site will work as a business.

As you work to create a new site that actually makes money, beware of these key mistakes, which I've witnessed more times than I can count. You'll profit by avoiding them.

MISTAKE #1:
"If We Build It, They Will Come"

Whether you're creating a site or rebuilding an existing one, don't ever assume that people will find it just because it's good. You need to work at bringing people to it.

Unless you already have a big user base or email list, you'll need to combine some SEO and marketing if you want people to get engaged with you online.

As I mentioned in section one, it's important to understand the basics of long tail keywords and meta tags to make your site search-engine friendly. But it's a good idea to push your SEO knowledge a higher level than that.

You can start by getting familiar with Google's keyword tool. Site owners who don't use the tool have a tendency to think they're doing better than they really are. They rejoice because their site is ranking #1 in Google for a specific term. But when you get them to take a look at the keyword tool, they realize they're winning top ranking for a phrase that draws almost zero traffic.

In the keyword tool, you can see how many

sites are trying to win for each term in Google's results. As counter-intuitive as it may seem, you should generally focus on keywords or phrases with at least some competition. Having some competitors tells you that others out there have found that they make money from the people who visit their sites after searching for these terms. If you pick a word or phrase and find in the keyword tool that nobody is trying to rank #1 for it in Google, it may just not be a desirable term.

The Google keyword tool is available here: http://www.googlekeywordtool.com/. It's interesting (a sometimes a bit bizarre) to see exactly what people out there are searching for. The tool, which is free to use, can also provide an almost bottomless well of great ideas on what to write about to if you want to draw traffic.

*<u>Tip #1: before you check traffic for any terms in the keyword tool, unclick "broad"</u> on the left side of the tool page and click the check box next to "exact." You'll then get

much more accurate results.

*<u>Tip #2: Don't worry too much about keywords</u> in the meta tags on your pages. Google doesn't look at them much anymore. Keywords in the content and the headline are much more important. What is important within your page's meta information is the page title and in the description. It's a good idea to put some real focus on the description, as it's often the thing that Google displays to people when your site page comes up in search. As such, it's an important "tease" to get people to click through to your site.

Links

Links are the true key that Google and the other search engines use to determine which sites will rank highest, and they're becoming more, not less, important. The underlying idea is that if lots of blogs and other sites link to your site, you're an authority. That's because, in Google's view, when others link to you, they're effectively putting their reputation on the line to recommend you to their readers.

This is another area where thousands of hucksters play tricks to try and get better search engine rankings. You can buy thousands of links for $5, pay consultants who operate a network of "quality" sites to give you links, trade links or do any number of other things that will allegedly elevate your profile in Google.

My advice is: don't do any of these things. Google has become much more aggressive about punishing sites that use link schemes, and they've also begun to weigh social media likes and links more heavily than links between sites. Produce good pages that people want to link to, and you'll be much better off.

*Tip: Don't forget internal site linking. Having a page called the "sitemap" with links to all your other pages is important, because it makes it easier for search engines to "crawl" your site and index all the pages. You also want to have what's known as an "xml sitemap" that gets submitted directly to

Google Webmaster tools, so the search engine knows about all your pages. Many of the available CMS systems have a plugin or feature that handles xml sitemap submission automatically.

Marketing

Whether you're launching a site or a feature like an email newsletter, social media page or mobile app, always remember that people usually don't sign up for something or make purchases in large numbers just because it's there. Even if you have limited resources, you need to create at least a basic marketing plan if you want to accurately gauge how much response you can get. This can range from paid advertising or email promotion to something as basic as testing various positions and colors for signup buttons on your site to see what works best.

The good news is that it's possible to test user response to a new product with a very small investment in Google AdWords or new options that are being offered with Facebook and Twitter advertising. The goal of just about everyone in this game is to create a "virtuous cycle," where you get $1.50 back for every $1.00 you put into marketing. It can take a lot of work to hone a marketing method down this way, but if it works you can potentially have a good-sized business on your hands.

Building things tends to be more fun than marketing them. But if you don't follow through and promote whatever you've created, you're not giving yourself the best chance of success. I've seen dozens of sexy new features wither and die because site owners didn't want to focus on the work of driving people to them.

MISTAKE #2:
"More Is Better"

There are so many things you can add to a website that it can — and does — make people's heads spin. Image galleries, forums, audio streaming, video sections, social media widgets…by the time this book is in your hand somebody will have invented even more.

Throwing too many options at your readers poses real problems, though. If you put lots of special sections on to your site, for example, you need to be ready to keep them all filled with fresh content or your reader will find lots of out of date information that makes you look bad.

Video seems to be a favorite thing for publishers to add to sites and then not follow through on. There's an endless parade of sites out there with big home page promos for video sections. When you click on them, you find that the "section" is comprised of one video that was made in 2009. That doesn't get people excited – it makes them wonder if you're still in business.

Comment boxes are another common dead zone. If you don't publish the kind of content that people want to comment on (which is to say, controversial things people like to argue about) you can end up with an empty comments box on every one of your pages. It's a red flag that gives everyone the impression that your readers aren't engaging with your site.

But there's a larger problem with piling too many gizmos onto your site. The more pictures, logos, promo boxes, widgets and other stuff you add, the longer it will take for your pages to download. Slow-loading pages are a big turn off to readers. But they can also hurt your search rankings. Nowadays, "site speed" is something that Google watches closely. The company's SEO mouthpiece Matt Cutts has announced several times that pages that download slowly will drop in SERP rankings.

Keep your site layout simple, and only add things that you're willing to update and maintain properly. Your readers and your search engine positions will both benefit.

MISTAKE #3:
"If We Get Lots Of Traffic, We'll Obviously Make Money"

A truly amazing number of people have given

me a puzzled look when I've asked them exactly, and I mean *exactly*, how their new website is going to make money. Once upon a time, I was just like them.

A website I built many years ago, but which I no longer work on, still gets about 50,000 pageviews per month. In peak months, it can draw over 100,000 pageviews. How much money does that site make? Virtually zero.

How can that be? Well, it's because I built it before I knew what I was doing. I'll offer it to you as an example of how NOT to proceed.

The site is about Irish culture, a topic I'm interested in because my own family heritage is Irish. People who are planning to visit Ireland tell me all the time that they've visited my site, and there are lots of Ireland-related keyword terms you can put into Google that will cause it to come up in the top three results. But it doesn't earn me more than pocket change for a simple reason: it wasn't *designed* to make money.

The site was built to draw people to my interest in Ireland. I didn't think it through much beyond that. After it started to draw a good deal of traffic, I tried to add in advertising, book publishing, paid newsletters and all sorts of other things to make money. None of them worked, because the site's basic information setup, layout and reader targeting were not explicitly designed to sell anything. It's also not in a subject category where Google pays a high cost per click through AdSense.

I traveled the classic blogger's path from pure enjoyment, at first, of writing about a topic I love to viewing the site as a pure nuisance just two years later. The lesson is this: Don't try to be Facebook by building a site and then attempting to come up with a way that it can make money. Get a clear vision of exactly how and where your site will generate revenue before you build it, or it probably won't make enough money to justify the effort you put into it.

I have another site that drives people to fill out an inquiry form to learn about buying life insurance. Every time someone fills out a form I get about $15. It gets a fraction of the traffic my Irish site does, but it makes money. That's because it was designed to move readers toward an action that I get paid a solid fee on. The content isn't just about insurance in a general sense. It's written to people who have already decided they need life insurance, and are in the process of choosing which company they will buy it from. If you build a site around a reader action that pays like that, you have a real chance of success.

Examples of sites designed to drive revenue:
http://searchengineland.com/: An SEO news site that does a nice, basic job of highlighting an invitation to follow on social media or sign up for a newsletter on every page at the upper right. It's almost hard for a reader to get away without signing up for something. The very dense home page also does a great job of pushing you to start clicking around right

away. That's important because this site makes money via advertising. The more pages you click on, the more they profit. All those newsletter signups draw people back to the site again and again to generate pageviews and ad impressions.

https://www.google.com/: Google is so familiar to us all that it may seem silly to list it here. But most web publishers, in my opinion, completely fail to pay attention to what makes it so successful. The opening page is brutally simple. You can't do anything but start searching for answers to questions. That's exactly what Google wants you to do, because they earn revenue by showing you ads that relate to all the words you type into the search box. Over the years, sites like Facebook, Tumblr, Pinterest and others have all come to take this Spartan design approach. It may not be feasible for all businesses, but it offers a good lesson in the fact that if you want to make money online, you need to have a focus on pushing people toward the action that results in a profitable transaction for you.

MISTAKE #4:
"We've Got To Have Everything Our Competitor Has On Their Website"

It's a great idea to look at all the sites in your competitive set to find ideas you might use on your own site. But don't assume that all your competitors really know what they're doing. Publishers large and small tend to go into a panic when they see that a competing site has added something new that they don't have.

I worked with one publisher whose eyes popped out of his head when he saw that a competitor had added a forum with all kinds of photo and video upload functions that would allow readers to talk to each other. He immediately wanted the same thing on his site, in spite of the high cost of building it. But a closer look revealed that almost nobody was actually using the forum. Within a few months, in fact, my publisher's own salespeople were making a point of showing that forum to clients to prove that the competitor had poor reader engagement.

Moral: your competitors may not be as smart as you think. If you see that one of them has added bigger pictures or some special new function, take a deep breath and ask yourself if you think it is actually going to make them any more money. You'll be surprised how often you can figure this out with pure common sense. Don't imitate anything they do until you feel convinced that it's actually driving revenue to them.

MISTAKE #5:
"We Have No Competition"

People often seem to feel that they must come up with an exotic, totally original idea in order to succeed on the Internet. But experience has taught me this: If you're thinking of a new online concept and when you look around, you see that no one is doing anything even slightly similar to it, hold your horses for a minute. Then ask yourself if the reason nobody else is doing it might be that there's no market for it.

Being first is a double-edged sword. Do you

remember Magellan or MySpace? They were the pioneers in search and social media. Both of them flamed out, only to be surpassed by Google and Facebook, who were not completely original, but did a better job of refining certain ideas. I don't mean to say that it's not a good to try new ideas. But I do suggest that if you want a high likelihood of a positive return on your business, get into something where you see clear proof that there's already at least some buying, selling or advertising activity online in your chosen category.

On a more advanced level, it's also good to remember that the web has a funny way of exploding competitive sets.

Particularly if you're working on a big or "category killer" type idea, think about competition that might come from "outside" your business. What does that mean? Well, in 1990, record companies all thought they were competing against other record companies. They never dreamed that by 2010, the #1 retailer of music on earth would be Apple, a computer company that doesn't own a single recording studio (I could name other similar scenarios, but I think Apple or Google would be named the culprit in almost all of them).

If you have a site about men's health, you'll have to compete for advertising dollars with sites that use other topics from fashion to football to reach men. Of course, this can work in your favor as well. If your men's health site becomes popular, you may be able to go out and get advertising from sports, fashion, dating and other secondary categories that interest men.

MISTAKE #6:
"We've Got To Have The Next Big Thing"

One of the truly nerve-wracking things about the digital world is that every month, it seems like something is going on that qualifies as "the next big thing." And not having a piece of the next big thing can make you feel very left out.

For the past 18 months or so, the next big thing in publishing has been the iPad, though it has now evolved into a broader category that includes many different types of tablet computers.

As soon as a few companies in the publishing business built tablet apps in 2012, it seemed like everyone else decided there was something wrong with them if they didn't have one. This set off an app-building rush that was more about trying to have an image of being forward-thinking than having any real idea of how to make money on an app.

It's easy to lose money by being too much of a "big new thing" pioneer. I recently worked for a client on the creation of an iPad app that cost over $35,000. That was actually a low fee, because tablet apps were such a new concept that the big guys – the *Wall Street Journals* and *New York Times* of the world – were paying hundreds of thousands for their tablet apps.

But before the app was even completed, the

game changed dramatically. HTML5 came along. It's a markup language that makes basic websites look great on mobile devices without any app being created, and it made the whole idea of building an app suddenly questionable.

On top of that, the price of building apps dropped like a stone. Just after completing our $35,000. app, I found that a development company with an online portal was offering the same thing, albeit in a less customizable form, for less than $3,000. The client I worked with suddenly didn't feel so great about having been the first in their niche to invest in the hot new thing.

Moral: If you think you can really make money on a hot new thing, go for it. Otherwise, consider that it might be better to sit back for a bit and watch your competitors act as guinea pigs.

MISTAKE # 7:
"A Slick-Looking Site Is What Really Matters"

If you run a high-end professional office or very expensive retail business, a very sharp, expensive-looking site may be in your interest. And if you want to sell banner ads to major advertisers, the visual "environment" of your site will need to be attractive.

But it can be a different story if you're trying to sell things on your site or drive leads. In fact, some direct marketers have told me without hesitation that "ugly sites convert best." The reason is that simple, more basic web layouts can not only drive readers to a desired action more effectively – they can also do a better job of conveying real personality than a site with a very "corporate" look.

You probably won't set out to build an ugly site no matter what I tell you. But keep in mind that one appeal of the internet is that it allows people to find places where they can get information from a qualified individual rather than a mega-company. Quite a few bloggers have built good-sized audiences in recent years with sites built on Wordpress themes that, while not exactly ugly, are pretty underwhelming graphically.

Flash introductions, videos that play with sound when the site opens, fancy typefaces and other adornments can look great when you open a site for the first time. But by the time you visit the site for the 5th time, they become irritating distractions.

Rather than go crazy over the graphic presentation of the site, I suggest you keep images under control (one big picture can often have a bigger impact than 10 small ones) and worry more about providing a navigation structure that makes it easy for visitors to find your most important content.

MISTAKE #8:
"The Designer (Or Developer) Can Figure Out How The Site Will Look"

If you want to get a site that matches your vision, don't ever assume that a developer or even a web designer can create it from a brief verbal description by you. Particularly if you're not comfortable with web terminology, it can be tough for them to translate what you say into a concrete site structure. Draw them a picture, or have someone draw it for you.

Smart companies make a spec design of the site that goes several pages deep, so that everyone on the business side can agree on it before it goes to a developer. This approach is just as valuable if you are a smaller businesses or content publisher, because it forces you to organize and codify your site concept before you actually start to build or re-work it.

What you need to draw out – and what's hard for a designer or anyone else to create for you – is a clear map of what you want someone to do when they get to your site. Ask yourself what is the one thing you want people to click on more than anything else when they come to your home page. Then where do you want them to click to from there?

It's not particularly hard to figure this out if you just start from the place people buy whatever you sell and then trace backward to the home page. But if you don't go through this exercise, you may end up with a layout that has your most important offer buried in a place where nobody can find it.

If you're an individual publisher, go ahead and simply do the most detailed hand drawing of the site structure that you can before it gets built. It's a worthwhile exercise, even if you are the one who is going to be building it.

*Tip: Don't Think The Home Page Is All That Matters: A very, very typical mistake in website design is to put a huge amount of thought and effort into the home page layout, and pay zero attention to how all the other pages on the site will look. This is a big error, because it's typical for 75% or more of all visitors to find your pages in search, and enter your site somewhere other than the home page. In fact, you should assume that a majority of your readers may never even see your home page. That's why you need to make sure that your most important offers, registration promos or sales icons are designed into all your site pages, so you can be sure all your readers will see them.

MISTAKE #9:
"I Took A Quick Look At The Statement Of Work And Signed It"

This is a hazard that comes up for mid-sized businesses or publishers, who have the budget to hire a marketing or development firm to upgrade a site.

If you're hiring an outside developer, make him or her give you a very detailed statement of work, and then go over it with a fine-toothed comb. Believe me, this is the point in the road where many projects become either big successes or miserable failures.

I've received statements of work from developers that include all kinds of additions I never asked for. If you see a charge for integrating video on your site that amounts to thousands of dollars, make sure to ask why it costs so much, and why you can't use a simpler approach. Do you really need to upgrade that mobile app so that it's perfectly compatible with the iPhone 5, when there's going to be another iPhone upgrade in just a few months? Sometimes when you push a developer to give solid reasons why a feature is necessary, you'll get surprisingly weak answers. Stick to your guns and don't buy into anything unless you're convinced that it's necessary.

Another key to avoiding trouble and controlling your project cost is to make sure you fully understand what you're expected to provide the developer with. Developers are notoriously vague about explaining client "deliverables," and it's a cause of much grief.

I once worked on a project where the developer told me we needed to provide "appropriate RSS feeds" to supply the content from our site to a mobile app. Unfortunately, I didn't ask exactly what that meant. As the project went along, it became clear that the developer expected me to provide several very specific types of RSS feeds that did not exist on our site. Creating them involved a big, separate job that made the overall project far more expensive and aggravating.

Ask your developer questions, and keep asking until you feel that you really understand what you need to bring to the project. Then make sure all those details are included in the statement of work before you sign it.

MISTAKE #10:
"Once It's Done, It's Done"

If you do things well, you can reasonably hope to use your website for 3 years or more without a major rebuild. But that doesn't mean you can simply walk away from it after launch.

It's inevitable that things will break down periodically. You or someone who works for you may upload some content incorrectly, causing the site to go down. Or you may find that, after using it for a few months, the CMS or email system needs some improvements.

Finally, things are always changing in the online world. 18 months from now, new options will exist that you may want to add to your site.

To keep yourself flexible and protected, get an agreement with your developer to provide ongoing service on your website. Alternatively, make a point of learning how to do more of the fixes yourself. If you use a hosting company that provides good service backup, you'll find that you can often fix problems by spending a little time on the phone with them.

4 Getting Even Smarter About The Web – Analytics, Email and Social Media For Non-Techies

"The Internet is just a world passing around notes in a classroom." – Jon Stewart

Web Analytics: Tracking your results

Website owners always obsess about how many pageviews they're getting. That's all well and good. But you can really benefit from looking at more than just pageviews, to get a little deeper sense of what your site visitors are doing. Even the simplest analytics tool can tell you a great deal about what is and is not working on your site.

First, here's a look at the three top analytics programs you're likely to come across:
Statcounter: A free program that's favored by many smaller publishers (though there is a

charge if you want to step up to their highest service level). Statcounter offers some great metrics that are hard to get elsewhere, though it lacks certain things too. With it, you can really see how individuals are travelling around your site with the "visitor paths" link. If you have affiliate links, you can see exactly how many people are clicking on each one and when they're doing so by looking at "exit links" and "exit link activity."

These are all great tools for figuring out exactly what's creating the most purchase or signup activity on your site. Statcounter also tracks which keywords are driving traffic to your site, though, curiously, it does not tell you how many unique visitors you have. Finally, it can tell you where visitors are coming in from – something I advise you to look at so you can understand, among other things, which links in your email newsletter people are clicking on to visit your site. Statcounter is pretty easy to install on just about any publishing platform.

Google Analytics: A free program that offers more and more sophisticated measurements all the time. I love the way it allows you to chart how an individual page is performing over time – a great tool if you have three or four very important shopping pages that drive most of your revenue.

GA has a sophisticated way of tracking site visitors all the way through to a purchase, which can be great for retail sites. It's not hard to put the code for this program on your site, but it can be challenging to configure some of its more advanced options. It offers unique visitor stats and just about everything else a fairly large company needs in analytics.

For some companies, it can be a good approach is to just set up Google Analytics and Statcounter, and use the best of both. Of the two, Google Analytics has a somewhat longer learning curve.

Omniture SiteCatalyst: Made by Adobe, is a super robust analytics tool that is definitely not free. It tends to be used by mid to large-sized companies who operate multiple sites and want the highest possible ability to measure visitor retention, do campaign testing, track subscription offer performance…you name it. Besides the fact that it's expensive and you need a developer to install it for you, an issue many people encounter with this program is that, unless there is a person who is assigned to work with it consistently, they'll never use more than 10% of its available functions. But if you're have a designated traffic guru or webmaster, SiteCatalyst can answer just about any question you can dream up.

*Tip - The most important metric that always gets overlooked:

Pageviews per visit. If you average less than 1.5 pageviews per visit, you're not keeping visitors on your site effectively. Getting better at this is often the best way to improve your online business. It doesn't matter how many new people you bring in if they don't stick around and spend time on your site.

*Tip - The metric people pay too much attention to:

Time on site. This may sound counter to what I just said, but time on site is a weaker measure of engagement than pageviews per visit. The problem is that, although analytics folks will tell you that there are controls in place to filter it out, if someone opens your website and then leaves it open while they go out for a walk, it's going to skew your "time on site" numbers like crazy. People leave sites open on their computers so frequently while the open another browser window that this metric, in my humble opinion, doesn't mean much.

Email – Never Underestimate It

Poor old email. It isn't sexy anymore. But the thing is – it works like crazy.

Have you noticed that when you sign up for LinkedIn, Facebook or Twitter, they start sending you a nonstop stream of email? That's because even these most cutting-edge companies know that email remains a powerful marketing tool. In fact, it may still be THE most powerful tool in the online marketing arsenal.

Email was once the only way to "capture" people who arrived on a website and then keep them engaged. Social media has changed that situation, to a degree. Nowadays you can set up ongoing communications with people by getting them to like you on Facebook or follow you on Twitter or other social services. But email is still the best option for some important reasons.

First and foremost, there's little doubt that people check their email constantly. Email is also less time sensitive than social media. Your tweets and even your appearances on other people's timelines in Facebook are good, but they're very perishable, and won't get seen much late at night or in the early morning. If you send someone an email at 10 am and they don't check their inbox until after lunch, they'll still see your message.

Email is great for engagement and sales

completion, two ideas that tend to merge together for some businesses. If your site is advertising supported, you may simply use email newsletters to keep getting readers to click back to your site to generate pageviews and see the ads. To accomplish this, make sure to show no more than brief introductions to your articles in your email, with an invitation to click and read the rest on your website.

Retailers are generally big users of email to promote new products or sales. They know it's easier to make a repeat sale to someone who has already purchased from you than it is to draw in a new customer. That's why you are bound to get lots of follow up emails from any retailer you buy from online.

I happen to believe that many publishers are too timid about sending out email. Hard core direct marketers know that people will tolerate far more email than most site owners realize. Many specialized publishers send something to their list every business day – anything from informational articles to product offers – and get consistent response with virtually no reader complaints. You can email people a great deal – as long as your messages include <u>real, useful information or a quality offer</u>. Bombarding them with vapid advertising will get you lots of unsubscribes.

Auto Responders: If you sell a single, somewhat expensive product like a membership or a multi-part course on how to speak French, you might want to take the course of having people sign up for some free introductory info, and then having an auto-responder send them a timed series of messages to bring them gradually toward the final purchase. Happily, there are now several applications available that allow you to do this cheaply and relatively easily. I personally like one called getresponse.com, which can also house your database of email addresses. You create a string of emails and the system sends them out automatically on a timed basis to anyone to signs up on your site. Getresponse can be a bit glitchy, but it offers a nice complete application to capture email signups, send newsletters to them and track how people are responding to you. It's not terribly expensive.

Consistency is a key to success with email, but it's hard to achieve. If you send one email and then don't follow up with another for months, people will forget who you are. Whatever type of emails you plan to send, make sure to set a rigid schedule or hire someone to send it out consistently. Otherwise, your email effort will lose steam fast.

Social Media: It's No Bonanza, But It's Very Important

Social media seems pretty simple when you approach it as an end user. But it presents subtle challenges when you try to use it as a tool to promote your business.

The issue with Facebook, Pinterest and Twitter, the three social tools that marketers have tried the hardest to infiltrate, is that people don't really use them to search for products, as they do with search engines. In fact, users of these services tend to have a negative attitude towards anything that looks or sounds like advertising. At the moment, Facebook advertising is my favorite option in the social media space. It offers you a very inexpensive way to get "likes" to your Facebook page. The trick is that you need to learn how to convert those likes into email signups, site visits or whatever else you consider your best tool to generate business from your website. Twitter's advertising option is newer and untested at the time of this writing, Pinterest doesn't sell advertising yet, though I'm sure they will eventually.

An approach that's has been more productive than paid advertising for many companies has been to approach the social media world more as a marketing opportunity. You can experiment in this direction by simply creating a personal page or a fan page, and then promoting the kind of content that gets people interested in you or your product. This is a much more gradual, multi-step process than search engine marketing, but it can be a good way to build an ongoing relationship with your target customers.

A brand that's succeeded brilliantly here is Chapstick. Their Facebook page is loaded with contests, articles about celebrities using their product and generally silly questions like whether men or women smile more. You won't find anything here about what's actually in Chapstick. But with 3.5 million likes, it appears that they've succeeded in giving their product a personality that people are attracted to. It is, however, hard to come up with the kind of light, frothy content around some other types of products, and it takes lots of energy and investment to keep generating promotions that bring people to your page.

If you want to get involved with Facebook, you should be aware that the rules on it seem to change every 15 minutes. One tool that can help you keep up with all the changes is a free email newsletter available at www.insidefacebook.com.

The odd thing about social media is that its biggest benefit may be the way it can help you boost your results in search engines. Google and Bing have both announced that they're basing their rankings more and more on social media activity. If you want to learn a great deal more about this process, I recommend you sign up for the course at linkliberation.com. It costs several hundred dollars and it's quite time-consuming, but it covers this in a broad marketing sense rather than focusing in on just one social media service. It's a complex area to get into, but it's definitely pushing aside traditional search engine advertising.

5 Three Golden Rules Of Online Success

"Where is all the knowledge we lost with information?" – T.S. Elliot

If you're like me, you'll find the business environment of the Internet fascinating. As you get more deeply involved in it, here are a few foundational thoughts that I believe can help make all your site launches more successful.

1) It's not how many people come to your site; it's *who* comes to your site.

If you want your site to produce revenue, work to attract the right people, not just a lot of people. That's particularly important if you sell via ecommerce or run an affiliate site. But in truth, it applies to almost all sites.

2) Beware Of Total Dependence On SEO

We all have our objections to Google's procedures. But like it or not, it's still the only search engine that really matters – the traffic you can get from Yahoo or Bing will be small potatoes by comparison.

But you should think about audience building beyond SEO if you want a business that's truly sustainable. Google is a fickle thing, and it's getting more fickle all the time. I've seen several publishers suffer traffic drops of more than 50% in the past year, and most have never really figured out why. If, like them, you build a business that's 100% dependent on search engine traffic, any time Google sneezes, your business will catch pneumonia.

Focus on building a <u>relationship</u> with an audience though your email list, social media sites and even offline venues, to insure that if Google turns off their traffic spigot to your site, your business won't simply drop off the map.

3) Never Let Perfect Be The Enemy Of Good Enough

It can be a big distraction to worry about making a site that's absolutely perfect. You never will. Microsoft built a billion dollar business by rolling out things that weren't really complete and then tweaking them gradually into a more finished state.

I always remember a quote I heard when I first got into this business: "The biggest enemy of the Internet economy is time." It's still true. If you let a web project drag on for months or even a year, some of the things you build will be obsolete by the time the site gets launched. Take the tools you've got available and get the site out there. Then watch how people react to it – and be ready to make continual improvements.

6 Reality Check: What Will And Won't Work With Advertising And Other Digital Business Models

"With no ads, who would pay for the media? The good fairy?" – Samuel Thurm

The mistakes that truly drag web businesses down over the long haul occur, I think, because creating a site forces most of us to do things we've never have done before. Building a website will force you to choose from a wide range of possible business models, develop an information strategy and then design an environment that channels the behavior of people toward a particular action (or transaction). Even the smartest, most experienced businesspeople, editors and retailers, in many cases, have no background in any of these things.

What follows here is a more in-depth look at two business model mistakes that seem particularly popular, and some ways you can avoid them.

BUSINESS MODEL FAIL #1:
"I Don't Really Have A Business Model, So I'll Try Advertising"

A big trap that both small and large companies fall into is deciding that it's going to be easy to make money through a business model they have no experience with, just because it's done online. Advertising is, without doubt, the most common example.

Online advertising can be profitable, but web publishers that go into it without "knowing the ropes" often work very hard at it, only to make a disappointing amount of revenue.

There are two main approaches to online advertising:

Google AdSense

This involves a simple process of signing up for an account, getting some code that will generate ads and pasting it into the back end of your site. Google's system reads the content on your site and generates, at least most of the time, ads that are related to what you're writing about. Google also tracks how many clicks you produce and sends you a check each month, based on how many times your readers click on one of their ads.

It's all very neat and clean, and doesn't involve that nasty business of selling ads to people live and in person, which is why so many online publishers are attracted to it. But AdSense only drives real revenue if you have the right kind of site.

You basically get a cut of the fee that the advertiser is paying Google for each click. And while there are a few categories that pay 80 cents or more for a click (some much more, in fact), a typical payout to the site owner is more like 15 to 30 cents per click. When you consider that no matter what kind of site you have, just a small percentage of your visitors will click on an ad, it quickly becomes obvious that you'd better have a whole lot of traffic if you want to make money with this approach.

The ultimate legend in this business is Plenty of Fish (www.pof.com), a dating site that's massively popular, particularly in Canada. Plenty of Fish was started by computer geek Markus Frind, who coded it from scratch simply to polish his programming skills. He got more than he bargained for. Mr. Frind now works a few hours a day, whiles away time on the world's best beaches and makes millions of dollars each year on what Google AdSense pays him for clicks to ads on his site.

It sounds wonderful, but there's a catch (pardon the fishing pun). Pof.com generates over 500 million pageviews a month. Most web site owners, even large, well-funded ones, never come close to having that much traffic.

A typical big company site generating a million pageviews per month or so will probably make only hundreds of dollars a month on AdSense. And the independent site owner with a 10,000 to 100,000 pageviews per month most likely won't make enough money in an average month to pay for dinner at a really good restaurant. Net net: AdSense is a great system. But if you want to make your livelihood through it, you need to focus on a topic that will draw very strong traffic. If you want to live on a more moderate level of traffic, seek out a topic category where the payout per click is higher.

A good way to start figuring this out is to sign up for a Google AdWords account. This is the other side of the service, where advertisers bid for clicks. You can start setting up some campaigns without actually buying anything, and in the process learn what people are paying for clicks on various keywords. Just remember that, as the publisher on the AdSense side who is displaying the ads, you get only a percentage of what the AdWords advertisers pay per click.

Traditional Display Ads: Selling Banners

If you're experienced in selling advertising and you're in a category where the top companies have real ad budgets, you can potentially build a nice business on banner ads. One thing that's nice about websites is that they can be good venues for both brand and direct marketing type ads, which is not true for many magazines and other offline venues.

I have a friend, an experienced ad salesman, who is co-owner of a site about mountain climbing. The site content is written by an editor who is a true expert on the topic, and has a good following of readers.

My friend the ad salesman signs banner ad contracts with companies who sell mountain climbing products. They pay a relatively high rate to advertise on the site because they want to attract an extremely narrow group of people who actually climb mountains. The site isn't making its owners into millionaires, but it earns them a reasonably good living and they get to work for themselves.

The rub with this kind of business is that if you don't charge a high enough rate (called a cpm) for your advertising, you'll never be able to defray the costs of creating content for your site. Producing content efficiently is skill that many small publishers have actually mastered better than the big guys. In most cases, major publishers have trouble focusing on the kind of content that drives transactions. As a result, they're still relying on print or broadcast revenue to pay for their editorial costs. As standalone products, their websites could never cover their content expenses and earn a profit from banner ads.

If you can create a site with good, unique content, attract a highly targeted audience and you happen to be in a category where people must buy something expensive (like mountain climbing equipment) to indulge an interest or business need, you may be in an online advertising sweet spot. But you need to have some experience in your chosen category, and you need to know how to call someone on the phone and sell them an ad.

*Tip: There are networks like ValueClick and Blogher that will place ads on your site and pay you for them. But they tend to pay very low cpm's. If you want to charge a good solid rate, you'll probably need to sell directly to advertisers.

Alternative Revenue Stream: Affiliate Marketing
Affiliate marketing allows you to make money from selling things even if you don't have your own products, or from helping advertisers collect leads. Most site owners start by signing up for an affiliate program with an intermediary like Commission Junction (cj.com), which will give you affiliate links to lots of different merchants.

Alternatively, you can open an account with a retailer that has its own affiliate program, or with a niche intermediary that focuses on affiliate programs in education or some other specialized category.

All these programs will give you text links or ads you can put on your site that include a tracking code. When someone clicks on them on your site and then completes a purchase or fills out an inquiry form, depending on the program, you get a commission. The payout is higher than what you get for a click on Google AdSense, but you only get paid if someone actually completes an action after they click the ad on your site. That's why these programs are categorized as "cost per action" (cpa) or "cost per lead" (cpl).

Both large and small operators have made considerable money in affiliate marketing. But you need to commit to it fully if you want to make more than pocket change at it.

The first online affiliate program that got popular was Amazon.com's. People recommended books on their site and got a percentage every time one of their site visitors clicked through and bought a book or something else on Amazon.com.

Most of them quickly encountered the main challenge of affiliate marketing: when you get paid a 4% commission (a typical payout on Amazon) on a $15. book, you're only making 60 cents per book. And $15. is an expensive book. At that commission rate, you must sell a huge number of books to earn a living.

This drives affiliate marketers to look for higher cost items to promote. Although commission percentages vary from one affiliate program to another, you'll just about always make more money selling $100. bathing suits than $6. books.

I've run several successful affiliate sites focused on "cost per lead" programs. They earn commissions by getting people to fill out inquiry forms for online degree programs, life insurance products and other things which are generally very expensive (or where, as the direct marketers say, the customer has a "high lifetime value"). I love the fact that I don't have to actually sell anything to earn a commission, and some of these categories pay a $15. - $25. per lead.

You'll encounter two main challenges in the cpa affiliate world. The first is that there are relatively few "high-payout" categories, and all the big direct marketing firms know what they are. Education and insurance, mentioned above, are both areas where you'll find tons of well-funded affiliate websites competing with you. You can do well against them, but only if you have a very clear and very narrowly targeted idea for a site.

The second challenge is a new one. In 2012, Google changed its search parameters (in the now famous "Penguin" update) in a way that, in the opinion of myself and others, favors large commercial sites (read: those who buy a lot of advertising from Google) over those of small publishers, particularly in the categories where a lot of affiliate marketing is done. Google says it's about showing its users better quality content, though that seems hard to believe when you look at the new results. However, it's a subject of much debate among SEO experts right now.

I can't prove anything about Google's methods, but I'll advise you be aware that the affiliate marketing environment has grown more difficult. If you want to get into it, start by doing lots of searches for the main keywords in your niche. See if Google is giving good rankings to sites that are similar to the one you want to create. It should give you a good sense of whether or not the category seems to be locked up by big players or some particular type of site.

*Tip: The affiliate program that offers the broadest possible number of options is Commission Junction (cj.com). Some higher end affiliate programs worth considering are vantagemedia.com and monetizeit.com. Be aware, however, that they tend to be selective about which sites they work with.

Selling Subscriptions To Instructional Products
If you're an expert on a subject, selling a subscription to a series of instructional videos or courses delivered via PDF or some other method can be a profitable business, whether

you're a small publisher or a large company with lots of resources.

This type of business is most powerful if you can teach something people need to make money or to perform some part of their job. A company I once worked with in the agriculture sector offered online learning tools about pesticides (fun topic!). Farmers received a certificate when they completed each "course." It made a great deal of money, because in many states, farmers must be certified to use these pesticides on their crops. If you can become an approved educator and provide certification like that, you can have a very nice business. You'll need to know people in the industry to succeed, however, as it can be tough to get a government agency or trade group to certify you in this role.

But online learning is a category with a great deal of growth potential. If you take a look at Lynda.com, you'll see that while tech is the biggest topic in online learning, people are also paying to learn things like how to take better pictures on their vacations, create excel documents and how to write marketing plans.

To draw in subscribers, teaching businesses like this rely heavily on email promotions and/or advertising. This topic is a bit outside the scope of website design. But I'll note that the site elements you need to have in place here include:

- A site that shows your content only to logged in, paying subscribers.

- A shopping cart that will accept credit card payments.

- A commenting form or other method that allows people to ask you follow up questions to your lessons.

- Most importantly, a customer service email or phone number where you are able to respond to your subscribers quickly, even to the point of cancelling and refunding their subscription quickly if that's what they want.

To get a sense of how these businesses work, sign up for a few of the free trial offers out there from online marketing gurus. You'll see how they use auto responders, follow up emails, videos and other promotional tools to drive prospects from initial interest to a purchase. You can try signing up for Link Liberation, which I've mentioned a few times, (http://www.linkliberation.com/fe/26445-from-the-ashes) not so much to buy the course, but to see how good they are at pulling you from an initial free signup to the point where you are ready to pay for their various products. Alternatively, sign up one of the free email newsletters from Ryan Deiss at http://drivingtraffic.com/ryan-deiss/. There, you'll see how a truly aggressive (perhaps a bit too aggressive in my view) online direct marketer works.

BUSINESS MODEL FAIL #2:
"I Can't Really Control What People Do After They Arrive At My Site"
It's pretty unlikely that you'll have much of an online business if people don't do something after they arrive on your site. As obvious as that sounds, it gets overlooked constantly. I

never cease to be amazed by how people show zero interest in discussing this issue during the website design process, and then immediately start having panic attacks about it as soon as the site is finished. "My website just doesn't do anything for me" is the #1 complaint I've heard from people in every imaginable business and profession. The reason their website isn't doing anything is that they're not doing anything to shepherd their site visitors to the right place.

Don't assume that if you don't sell anything over the internet, you don't need to influence the reader's behavior on your site. A "call to action" can be either "in your face" or very understated, depending on the nature of your business. But it's an element that has to be there, unless you want most of your visitors to look at a page or two and then leave without contacting you or remembering you.

Of course, you have to figure out what you want a reader to do on your site before you can promote it. Here are some approaches to reader engagement to consider for various types of sites:

A High-End Professional Office Website
If you're a lawyer, medical specialist or other professional providing an expensive service to a select group of people, the key role for your website may be to simply reinforce your image. You may even work from the assumption that most of your site visitors will be people you've already met in person and given a business card to.

But it's still a good idea to engage them, get them to read more about you and, most importantly, <u>remember</u> you. Make sure to have some good, recent content on your site, including articles you've written or informational pieces about how to deal with particular types of problems. If they come to find out about you as a real estate attorney, you may benefit if they spend enough time on the site to learn that you work in trademark law and handle contracts too. At the very least, make sure there is an option to contact your office, and that someone is paying attention to any inquiries that come in.

Remember that the metrics are actually in your favor. If you only get follow-through from a few of the right people, you may benefit handsomely. It's worth spending the time to build a good net, if the occasional fish you catch is a big one.

More Broad-Based Professional Office or Service
If you're a local real estate lawyer, acupuncturist or tax accountant who works with a broader number of people at a more modest price point, you'll want to actively solicit business through your website. It will be in your interest to work a bit harder to load up your site with content that will draw traffic from Google. Spending some time to learn SEO skills will be important, because you'll probably have competitors out there working hard for online attention.

The call to action can be more "up front" here, even if you don't close sales or collect credit card numbers online. Try to develop a good way of getting people to give you an email address, and then follow up with them gradually. Sending out a simple email newsletter or alerts about certain key issues can build their trust and interest in what you do. If you give them good information about new ways acupuncture can be used to deal with knee problems, for example, you can keep yourself in their minds until the time comes when those knees start hurting.

You Have A Physical Store, But Don't Sell Anything Online

Plenty of merchants use the web effectively even though they don't execute transactions online. Car dealerships, for example, work very hard to initiate the sales process online, because they know that it tends to lead customers to come in and complete a purchase live and in person.

Ecommerce, with its issues of packing, shipping and handling returns, may not make sense for you if you're not in a volume business. In that case, you want to focus 100% on a site that gets a visitor clicking around and learning what's unique about YOU, and which gets them to give you an email address so you can send them follow up offers that will draw them into the store. It's not complicated, but it's something that many storeowners work very hard at offline, and then fail to do at all on their websites.

Consistent messaging will make people feel like your store is a place where lots of good things are going on all the time.

Publication or Blog – Affiliate Marketing
Blogging is now one of the most popular activities on earth, because it's easy to get into and we all love to share our knowledge and express opinions. But remember that, as *The New York Times* once said of the blogoshpere, "Never have so many people written so much to be read by so few."

If you want to make money as an affiliate, focus your blog on a topic area where there are offers that pay a high cost per action. Then make an active effort to push readers to those offers. Don't just post articles and hope for the best.

Most affiliate sites make their money on a few key pages that help people through some part of the shopping process: best products, this week's sales, best priced, most highly rated, etc. You should aim to create some "consummation" pages like this with all your best affiliate offers on them. Then make sure that the top nav bar and lots of links in your articles drive people to these pages more than any of the others on your blog.

It's also a very good idea to test what is the most effective way of presenting offers. Try linking to them through text, and then try putting the links behind photos. Contrary to popular belief, I have found the photos don't necessarily always drive the most clicks. Make an organized effort to figure out what works best for you, and then keep on repeating it.

Businesses That Sell Physical Products Online
If you're a big retailer with lots of products, you're probably more likely to hire a team of people like me than read this book. For smaller companies, the best online approach is often to sell a limited but unique product line or, in some cases, just a single product like a book.

Businesses like this thrive by finding a way to offer customers a free "taste" of what they sell, and then drawing them gradually toward purchase. The website should be as uncomplicated as possible, but there needs to be a strong call to action.

Obviously, you need ecommerce capability to make a site like this work. That means being able to accept credit card payments and then actually ship the products. If you're just starting out in this business, the easiest approach is often to use PayPal as a "shopping cart" to complete your sales. Besides its simplicity, PayPal will usually collect an email address from each of your customers during the sales process. That's very important – you should build a list of customers and send follow up communications with them on a regular basis. People who buy something from you once are almost always your best prospects to sell to again.

It's often not that hard to figure out what your best approach is, as long as you start out with the attitude that you're going to focus on response and try a variety of approaches toward driving it. The clearer you are about that first thing you want a reader to do when they get to your site, the more successful you're likely to be.

Nowadays, people are used to seeing sites that drive them aggressively to everything from free signups to purchases. Don't be afraid to tell your site visitors where they should go to find your best offers.

7 Conclusion: Keep On Learning

"Technology offers us a unique opportunity, though rarely welcome, to practice patience." – *Allan Lokos*

To succeed on the web, it's extremely important to get comfortable with the idea that you never get much of a chance to coast. The minute you've got something figured out, everything changes and you've got to come up with a whole new way of operating.

The ways that we all consume information and communicate won't settle into a stable pattern anytime soon. In fact, they'll probably change at a more and more rapid rate. It's not at all hard to imagine, in fact, that websites will become totally obsolete at some point.

But it seems pretty likely that digital products

in some form will remain very important for most businesses. To stay in the race, your best bet is to become a lifelong student, not so much of technology, but of the ways we all use technology to communicate and do business with each other. The one thing I guarantee is that there will never be a dull moment.

To keep yourself ahead of the curve, I recommend that you get in the habit of reading as many articles and newsletters as you can about online business and marketing. Here are some that I've found helpful:

ezSEO Newsletter

http://ezseonews.com/
This free weekly email has long been one of my favorite info sources. Beyond SEO, it covers all kinds of topics in site building, managing your workflow, creating content for the small publisher and more. It tends to be angled toward affiliate marketers and those using AdSense, but it covers the site management waterfront really well. You'll find

lots of offers for paid courses in web marketing. You won't want to go crazy buying them all, but I have found a few that are quite helpful and reasonably priced. I built my very first site, in fact, by purchasing a guide here for about $100., and just doing exactly what it told me to. It resulted in a very profitable little business for me.

Search Engine News

https://www.searchenginenews.com/
This is for those who want to take a really deep dive into search engine optimization. Its newsletter is not free, but if you really want to work hard on your site traffic, it's an excellent guide.

Paid Content

http://paidcontent.org/
A free daily email. This is more about the concerns of larger media businesses. It's great, however, if you want to get a sense of which online startups are prospering, and how the major publishers are trying to make money on the web. For smaller publishers, it's a good

window into a bigger world. It will make you feel good to see that the big boys are struggling with many of the same problems you have.

Inside Facebook

http://www.insidefacebook.com/

A free daily email newsletter that covers every possible aspect of marketing on Facebook, as the title suggests. If you want to gain social marketing expertise, you'll be amazed to see how many changes are constantly occurring on Facebook.

Which Test Won

http://whichtestwon.com/

If you're a retailer and you want to start doing promotional offers online, this is a great website and free newsletter about how to drive real response to your offers. You'll find an ongoing series of tests on how changes in web page designs and landing pages affect the level of response you get, with real numbers on results. You can learn a great deal here – and find that what drives people to click on an offer can be quite different than what you expect.

SEOBraintrust / Link Liberation

http://seobraintrust.com/

SEO Braintrust / Link Liberation, which I've mentioned previously in this book, is the best thing I've come across for those who want to pull back from all the details of SEO, site design, email promotion and the like, and learn how to take a bigger picture view of digital marketing. The two guys that run this are very good at applying very classic marketing concepts that still ring true to the online environment, and they preach loud and hard that it's a mistake to depend too much on Google for your business – a view that I happen to agree with. SEO Braintrust has various free email news options, but you'll have to pay to get most of their training courses.

8 Appendix: Checklist Of Questions To Ask Your Developer

If you have the budget to hire a developer to work on your website, you'll get a better result if you do as much homework as you can in advance. Because every site design is different, it's not possible to come up with a "one size fits all" list. But the list below will provide at least some key questions you'll want to ask your developer no matter what you're building.

On a website redesign:

1) Are we staying on the same content management system (CMS) or going to a new one?

2) If a new CMS, who will train the site manager(s) to use it?

3) If a new CMS, will there be any significant change in the workflow involved in posting content to the site?

4) Will the new site have the same urls as the old one? If not, will all old urls be forwarded to the new ones so that no positions will be lost in Google?

5) Who will be designing the graphic appearance of the new site? What will the approval process be?

6) Will the new site be divided into content sections? If yes, do we have to tag old articles to fit into those sections or will they be carried over automatically? (If it's not automatic, this can be a huge job)

7) Will the site carry social media buttons? (Facebook, Google+, Pinterest, etc.)

8) What analytics program will we be using to measure traffic?

9) If site carries advertising, what ad serving platform will we be using?

10) How will we handle testing and correction of bug fixes during the launch?

11) How do we handle bug fixes or additions after the site is fully launched?

12) Will the site display properly in Explorer, Chrome, Safari and Firefox? (Explorer is almost always the problem one.)

13) Will the site pages download quickly? (A key user experience issue that can be tested in Google webmaster tools.)

14) Will the site have "responsive design" that makes it display well on smartphones and tablets?

15) Will the site submit xml sitemaps to

Google regularly, or will that have to be done manually (Automatic is obviously better. This is important for SEO traffic).

On the creation of a mobile application:

1) Will the tablet application work on all tablets or only iPads?

2) Will the phone app work on all smartphones or only on iPhones?

3) Do we need a different ad serving system for mobile devices?

4) Who will handle bug fixes and upgrades? (Important – if you don't have a developer lined up to do this it can be very hard to find one who is familiar with coding mobile apps.)

About The Author

Paul Mannet has worked for over 15 years in digital media as a publisher, business analyst and project director. He has helped entrepreneurs gain funding from investors, organized large business and tech teams to execute major website launches, and worked with smaller companies and individuals who want to make their sites more profitable.

Paul has created websites in over two dozen industries, gaining a deep understanding of the financial metrics of advertising, affiliate marketing, ecommerce, data sales, online education and virtually every other internet revenue model. Several of the sites he has worked on generate over a million dollars per year. He lives in Port Washington, NY and can be reached at publisher@irishletter.com